# These Women
# Better Get Smart!

Words to the wise
ascertained through
the experiences of Lula

Lula Lucritia Gayles Herring

SPG SELAH PUBLISHING GROUP

"To live in the hearts of our seventeen children
is not to die"

In Memory of
Lula Lucritia Providence Adams Gayles
and
Edward Cato Gayles ll

Edward Cato Gayles II        Lula Lucritia Adams Gayles

# Contents

# Contents

# Contents

# Contents

# Contents

# Contents

# About the Cover
# Lady in the Bathtub

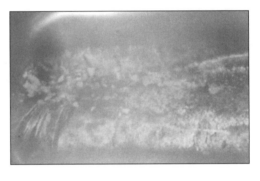

After taking a shower and trying to clean the bathtub three times with Ajax cleanser and not succeeding in getting rid of the residue, I decided to stop trying. I left the bathroom for about five hours and upon my return I saw the image of the lady in the bathtub. Knowing that no one would believe a description of the image, I grabbed the camera and took a picture. For years I showed only a few people the lady in the bathtub. Not knowing what to do with her I put her in the closet.

Years later I was watching a program on WNED–TV channel 17 in Buffalo, New York, featuring art works from the Toronto Museum and saw a picture of a fourteenth-century queen that resembled the lady in the bathtub. I ran and took her out of the closet and took her to the store and had her enlarged to poster size. It was then God revealed to me what the picture meant. As I looked closely at the picture I could see at least twenty-seven other images. God said to me, "The lady in the bathtub is you, you are the wealth and character of God, and not a devil in hell can touch you."

# Photographs

Photographs span seven generations starting with the generation of Millers, Weston, Adams, Gayles. Married names of the nine daughters of Edward Cato and Lula Lucritia Adams Gayles Davis, Suarez, Herring, Kee, Johnson, Floyd, Shaw, Livingston, Varner.

# Introduction

It is interesting, even fascinating, how words have changed and altered my attitude, mind, and even my life. Though words are not physical sticks and stones, whether subtle or abrupt, words can hurt or help, encourage or discourage, even take the best I can be and leave me robbed of my senses. Words can kill, steal, and destroy faith, hope, and love. Words can edify, build a righteous character, encourage, and influence. A simple yes or no can mean death or life.

I learned at an early age the significance of words by listening to those who have "been there," instructing me "how to get there." As a child, my uncle taught me, "Fool me once, shame on you. Fool me twice, shame on me." I learned not to be fooled twice. Mrs. Keel, my Sunday school teacher, observed something I was doing and said to me, "Lula, it's nice to be important, but it's more important to be nice." I don't remember what I was doing that caused Mrs. Keel to make this statement; however, I learned the importance of being nice. As a teenager on the back of the school bus I tried to fit in by swearing and cussing. Like a beginner the words were terribly discordant. On the way home my best friend Cynthia said, "That just doesn't sound like you, Lula!" I was so humiliated I never had the desire to swear again.

I remember the time I smoked a cigarette. I lit the cigarette, inhaled and exhaled, nothing, and then nothing. I never had a desire to smoke again.

I was engaged to be married at the age of twenty-two and my fiancé said, "Our first fight is when you pour my beer down the drain." I returned the engagement ring. I heard about a man and a woman who died of gas asphyxiation. The entire community turned out to see how the wife of the dead man and the husband of the dead woman would react at their spouse's funerals. "Curiosity seekers," the preacher called the audience. Several days later I said, "Mom, I don't ever want to die a shameful death." Mama said "Lulie, you know how you don't die a shameful death?" I said, "How, Mama?" Mama said, "You don't do anything shameful." Needless to say GOD has had mercy on me. I was sure of how I didn't want to die, but I was not sure of how I wanted to live.

I learned a lot from Mama, but I had not learned to accept Lulie for who she was. I learned to feel inferior. As I walked with my eyes to the ground at Jefferson Avenue and Best Street, an older dark-skinned black man with white hair rolled his car window down and said, "Girl, why you got yoe head down?" and he vanished. Why was I walking with my head down? As I walked home to 110 Timon Street and pondered the thought, "Girl, why you got yoe head down?" There was not an explanation other than I was a Negro and had been taught by society to hate my heritage, my color, and myself.

From that day on I was not going to ever belittle Lulie or think of myself as seeing black as anything but beautiful. I was going to have so much pride in myself that no matter what anyone said, I was better than the best.

Lula Lucritia Gayles Herring
Bennett High School

However, that was just beginning. My high school teacher asked a Negro student to read the definition of a Negro. The definition read on this wise Negro, black to purple-black skin, wide nose, thick lips, and kinky hair. As I heard the words I inspected my arms and hands. I saw none of what was being read. The schools gave misinformation; I found it necessary to learn about the Negro on my own.

Every day after leaving East High School I would go to work at Columbus Hospital, then I would go to the main public library on Washington Street searching for information about the Negro. I read about slavery and I thought slavery was something to be ashamed of—at least this is what society wanted me to believe.

I began to look at the Negro in the same manner I had looked at myself, walking with my head down. I realized that there was absolutely no reason to be ashamed. Africa had to abort some of her bravest, strongest, and most intelligent to dig out a new nation with brute strength, a nation that could not be called home. A nation that would ever tell the Negro to go back to where they came from. Back to their proud lands of Africa from where they were kidnapped, raped, dehumanized, culturally stripped, bound, gagged, and dragged into the developing of the United States of America.

In spite of the pride, I fell prey to racism when I learned of the lynching of Emmett Till in August of 1955. Emmett was a fourteen-year-old boy who was accused of whistling at a local white woman. He was beaten and mutilated by the Ku Klux Klan and his body thrown into the Tallahatchie River. All that I had experienced, heard, and read about the Negro incited my most vulnerable sense of uselessness. I woke up one morning and realized I was consumed with the very ideas of hatred I so vehemently detested in others. I prayed to rid my thoughts of the hatred and prejudice in my heart. GOD healed me of racism and prejudice.

My thoughts turned to exploring the tactics men used to seduce women to respond on command. In 1977, I began to write my thoughts and feelings on pieces of paper, realizing love improperly handled could cause a Christian to crumble and fall.

I could not understand why I could not complete *These Women Better Get Smart,* then it dawned on me: *I* had not gotten smart. I used to hear my brothers' girlfriends complain to Mama about how my brothers would not pay them the attention they desired. Mama would always say, "These women better get smart." Regardless of the complaint, whatever the reason, Mama would admonish the woman to "get smart." I always thought it was other women who had to get smart, until I realized *I* was not smart. It took the experiences of life for me to get smart.

Mama and Daddy were not worldly people and were not aware of most of the tactics men used to manipulate women into ungodly submission. A wife was to obey the husband. I did exactly that until I realized that GOD was a husband who would not ask me to do anything wrong. I divorced the notion of obedience to the will of the flesh and my soul was arrested, dedicated, and submitted to the will of GOD.

If there is one message I could give to women it would be this: love yourself so much that when someone asks you to do something against your principles, don't compromise your integrity. Tell them, "I can't oblige you," and keep stepping. Don't settle for an abusive two-cent man when you can wait for a loving million-dollar man. It is my endeavor that through the reading of *These Women Better Get Smart*, women and men everywhere will recognize "You have a brain, use it! You have a heart, don't lose it."

# A Prayer of Meditation

Lord, I thank You for the luxuries in my life at 122 Brunswick Blvd. When I think of 325 South Division Street in Buffalo, New York, I think of chinches, rats, roaches, bedwetting smells, and a bucket in the closet being used as a toilet. Sleeping in a fourteen-foot room, probably six feet wide, with eight people. I remember sharing a bunk bed and looking at old wallpaper hanging from the ceiling. I can remember polishing toilet water bottles from G.C. Murphy's. Competing for the food with the roaches, afraid of reopening a box of cereal, waiting for the bathroom.

Seldom did we have sweets. As I savored the last drops of the Eagle Brand milk from a can, I came upon a lump. Pulling the can from my lips, I looked with disgust and threw the can as far into the alleyway as I could. The last savoring drop was an adult female roach.

Bras were worn until they turned gray, tattered, and torn. Twisting the runs in the stockings so no one could see (so I thought). Panties stained and torn, elastic stretched (a knot will fix that).

One thing I do remember, there was more love, singing, and sharing something I thought every family possessed. My friends would bring their friends to see the circus of roaches as they marched up and down the walls. When some of my friends went home, there were no roaches and, unfortunately, in some cases no love.

Fredrick, George, Edward, Eleanor, Rosa, Edna, Lula
515 Clinton Street

I believe and know the secrets that man desires are in the Word—be it wealth, youth, positions, politics, guidance, comfort, wisdom, understanding, love, coping, how to, what to, when to, where, why, how, if, should I, could I, and would I?

George, Ronald, Stanley, Vivian, Diane, Edward, Kenneth, Edna, Pamela,
Fredrick, Steven, Gregg
Lula, Eleanor, Lula (Mama/Mamo), Rosa, Marian, Alice
My Family
The Gayles Family Singers

*These Women Better Get Smart* are words of wisdom I learned from observing and listening to Mama and the people in and out of the photos. Whether young or old, I never met a person from whom I did not learn something profitable. Everyone I encountered taught me what not to do or what to do.

# Freedom

Tears are the relief of the soul.

Marc Steven Herring (my youngest son)

# If Time Stood Still

You young innocent being,
    looking and not seeing.
If you had known
    where you were going,
    would you be here?

Buffalo Zoo

# Revolutionized

The mere words from my lover's lips
    made my heart melt.
Those same lips formed my wilting heart
    into a shape so rigid,
        the sharpest dagger could not penetrate it.

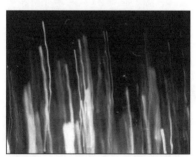

Dark Room University @ Buffalo

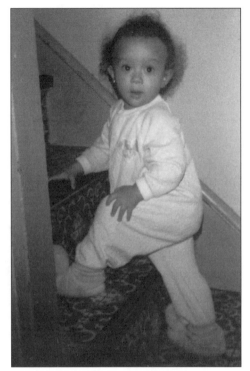

Tiara Diamond Herring
(my granddaughter)
122 Brunswick Blvd.

## Shoes

Shoes are made for going places.
Depending on where you want to go
    the  appropriate shoes will
    get you
    to that destination.
Those who intend to stay at home
    wear house shoes.

# Alternatives

When I cry over the loss of one thing

Janet (Fatima), Dottie, Roy, Bernice

I find consolation in knowing
I have one or more things
I have not lost.

Rosie, Diane, Vivian, Pam, Edna

# Searching

Love comes in many colors.
Now that we have found one another, as we depart
let us not forget to hold this time of love in our hearts.
When clouds get dark and days are drear,
remember the love we all felt when we were here.

Bumbo, Aaron, Buttons, Poppy, Rachel, Mia, Faith, Vivian, Diane, Jennifer
Bryan, Marion, Linda
(Nephews, nieces, sisters, son & daughter)

# Florida

The fountain of youth
has been discovered
in the minds of the elderly.

Grandpa (my great grandfather)　　Maa (my great grandmother)
515 Clinton Street

For Better
or for Worse

Cousin Annie, Maa

If I stay on my side of the road
and you stay on yours
fortunately or unfortunately
our paths will never cross.

Says Who?

Lulie, Rosie
First Shiloh Baptist Church

Thoughts without actions
Bring forth no artifacts.

Lulie
325 South Division Street

## Lady-killer

From a seed,

to a cultivated flower
from a flower,

to a dead root is
man's delight.

Lulie
498 Spring Street

Lu La
122 Brunswick Blvd.

## Exercise Thought

Heather, Tiara (granddaughters)
122 Brunswick Blvd.

When I care what you think
I do what you say.
When I think not to care
I do what I think.

# Sweat

The more I learn
the more I realize
how little I know.

Miss Thad (Bubba Miller's wife)
Maa, Bubba Miller (my great uncle)
515 Clinton Street

Uncle Benny's motorcycle
(Maa & Grandpa's son) 1929?

# Gatekeepers

Life could be what you make it
if it weren't for others making the decisions.

Rachel Bunch (my niece)
Foreign Mission, Sabana Grande LaBoya, Dominican Republic
July 2002

# Skin Deep

A beautiful face may reflect love.
However, a beautiful body reflects discipline.

George, Lula
First Shiloh Baptist Church

Sculptor, Marion Gayles Shaw

# Disorder

Sing to the soul
and to the spirit
of the people,
and not to their flesh.

David V. Herring (my second son)
Marc Steven Herring, Artist
122 Brunswick Blvd.

The Root
of It All

Individually they are tossed about
trampled underfoot
moreover, scattered back and forth.
Collectively, they
form a cohesive tower
of strength.
Tons of pressures have crashed
against them.
The results, a partial tear.
They speak with
one unanimous voice
and seldom find the need
to speak twice.

Mr. & Mrs. Peter Weston (Maa and Grandpa)
Married August 18, 1887 South Carolina, Richland County
(Great grandparents, grandparents, mom, great aunts, great uncles,
great aunts, aunts, uncles, cousins, sisters, & brothers)
by the Rev. James Scott
60th wedding anniversary, April 1948
515 Clinton Street

Keep the Pace

Some people think step by step.
Others think
down
the
road
and

around the bend.

## Applicable

What we gain in life
is not always useful.
What we achieve in life
is not always profitable.

Steve, Beedo, Whammo

# Is Once Enough?

There are those who are happy
because it happened once.
There are others that are unhappy
because it will not be repeated.

Evangelist Lula Lucritia Gayles Herring leaving for foreign mission to
Sabana Grande LaBoya, Dominican Republic
122 Brunswick Blvd.

# Needle in a Haystack

Some people wait a lifetime for happiness.
Some people never obtain it.
Others gain it, yet know not how to use it.
Still others gain and lose it,
while others obtain and increase it.

Lu Gal
Darien Lake Orchard Park, New York

# Upward Mobility

There's more to life
than poverty.
Graduate!
Get out of grammar school.

Junnie, Fred, Kenny, Santa Claus, Buddy
Sattler's, 998 Broadway

# Should I, Could I, Would I?

Have you ever wanted to,
Knew you really shouldn't,
went ahead and did what you wouldn't
or
not because you couldn't
followed better judgments
and restrained doing what you shouldn't,

yet
longed to
because
you
wouldn't.

Aaron Gayles (my nephew)
Gayles Beauty Supplies
1380 Jefferson Ave.

45

# Dissatisfied, but Not Restrained

Take what you can get
for the moment
and at the same time
pursue
what you really want.

Gregg Gayles, "ah, ga, man" Edna
Mac Alpine Presbyterian
2700 Bailey Ave.

*Exodus*

Rosa Lilly Salisbury Gayles, Uncle Jacob Gayle
(Grandma Rosa, Daddy's mother)
Willert Park Projects, Jefferson Ave.

I am not afraid of graying.
I am not afraid of growing old.
I am afraid of dying
Before I am cold.

# Don't Bother

It takes an attraction
to get my attention.
You have neither the attraction
nor my attention.

Aunt Lu Gal
122 Brunswick Blvd.

# Where Is?

A husband is:
someone
without
hands,
feet,
eyes,
and
ears. He has a wife!

Dabo, George, Munchie, Bumbo, Christopher, Bryan,  Michael, Marc
(sons and nephews)
122 Brunswick Blvd.

F
a
i
l
u
r
e

Down
is
perfectly

straight.              Marc E Phooh
                      122 Brunswick Blvd.

# Which Way to Go?

If I meet with opposition going in one direction,
I will change my direction.
If I meet with opposition in every direction,
I will change my strategy.

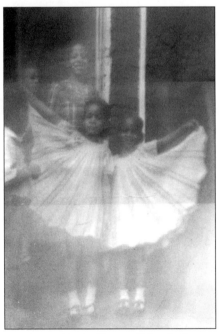

Junnie, Rosie, Eleanor, Edna, Lulie
(Edna and Lulie wearing dresses Mama crocheted)
325 South Division Street

# Thought You Took It, Didn't You?

Thought you took my body
brought it under subjection.
Thought you took my mind
wiped it clean as a slate.
The only thing you didn't take
was what you couldn't see.

Lulie, Edward, Edna, Eleanor, Ronnie
Rich Stadium, Orchard Park, New York
Buffalo vs. Miami Dolphins (Buffalo won)

# In Your Presence

Gracious Lord:
We come to you as humbly as we know how.
Lord, we are asking you to come the more into our lives
Lord, we are seeking you to create within us a clean and a pure heart.
We recognize and understand that we are in your presence and as the Holy Spirit gives utterances we know that the ground we are standing on is Holy Ground. It is with great assurance that we know, we are in your Holy Presence.
With much Agape.

Tiara
122 Brunswick Blvd.

# Top of the Page

Shelly-my-belly, ooh-be-do, Melanie Noodles
(nieces and goddaughter)

Success is never at the bottom.

# Who's Wrong?

What's wrong with a man
is a woman.
If it wasn't his mama, his sister, his aunt or his
girlfriend
some woman told him his stink don't stink.
What's wrong with a woman is her love for a man.

Audrey, Mia, Shelly, Carmen, Vincent, Faith, Barus
(nieces and nephews)

# Face It

Wrinkles are the skin's inability
to stand up any longer.

Matha (Mama's mother and midwife), (Stanley)
110 Timon Street

Each time Mama was ready to deliver a baby, Motha would send us outside to play. Then the doctor came to the house carrying a black bag. Every time the doctor would leave, a new baby brother or sister was left, so I thought the baby was in the black bag the doctor carried.

# Do Unto Others

How we treat ourselves
and intermingle with others
discloses how we feel about ourselves.

Nathan, Tiara (grandson, granddaughter)
122 Brunswick Blvd.

# Circle or Square

People like you
for who you are.
Not for who
they can create.

Lu Gal
122 Brunswick Blvd.

# Destruction

Walls—like relationships—are harder to rebuild
once they have been torn down.

Ramsey, Pharaoh (nephews)
122 Brunswick Blvd.

# Father of Mankind

Dear Lord,
Why should I be cursed?
Why give me a mind
    that my body can't utilize?
Why not give all the brilliant minds to men?

Tiara, DaDa
(granddaughter and grandson)
122 Brunswick Blvd.

# Spirit and Truth, Not Flesh

It is humanly impossible
to please GOD.

Bry-yo, McDuffy, Marc–e-pooh, Dabo
(friend)
122 Brunswick Blvd.

# Revelation

Captured in picture
is the prophecy
of death.

Lula, Lula (Mamo)

# One Life to Live

I love the man I married.
The man I love is married.
If something were to happen to the man I love,
I could not marry him because he has a wife.

Lula, George
122 Brunswick Blvd.

# Better Than the Best

I don't compete with others,
rather I compete with myself.
Considering I am a better judge
of who I can be
and what I can achieve
through Jesus Christ.

Mamo, The Gayles Family Singers
Tiara
122 Brunswick Blvd.

# Remove the Threat

In quietness and meekness,
greatness is made greater.

First row from the bottom: Edna, Cousin Vivian, Cousin Junior, Cousin
Aaron, Lulie, Junnie, Rosie, Buddy, Fred, Eleanor. Second Row: Uncle David,
Cousin Wesley, Cousin Amy, Mama, Tonto (son), Uncle Julius. Third row:
Cousin Lewis, Cousin Helen, Bubba Jack (great uncle), Annie Gussie, Papa
(great father), Motha (great mother). Fourth row: Cousin Edna, Aunt Dora
(great great aunt), Bubba Miller (great uncle). Top row: Grand Pap & Maa
50th wedding anniversary
Four generations of Miller Adams Gayles Family
First Shiloh Baptist Church   South Division Street

# If We Care

We as parents cannot expect the schools
    to do all the teaching and
    the churches to do all the preaching.
We have the responsibility to our children
    that can never be nurtured outside the family.

Top row: Annie Gussie, Bubba, Jack, Uncle John,Cousin Vivian, Matha,
Papa, Uncle Paul, Peaches. Bottom row: Uncle Julius, Uncle David,
Norma Jean, Junior
Technical High School  presently City Honors

# Compliments

When I lose what I had, everyone tells me.

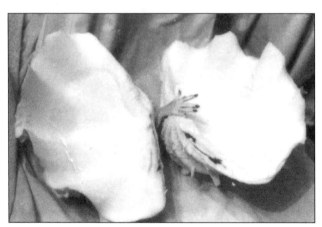

University @ Buffalo 28 Main Street

# Aspirations

Men have not necessarily failed
    for women to want to achieve.
Fortunately, women too are human.

Lulie, George
Memphis, Tennessee

# Beauty Is Skin Deep, Says Who?

Skin encapsulates beauty.
Beauty penetrates the skin's surface
and radiates.

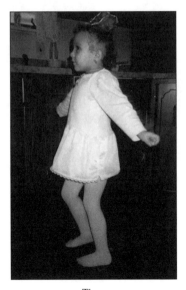

Tiara
122 Brunswick Blvd.

# Found and Lost

Just because you have it,
    doesn't mean it's yours to keep.

Rosie, Eleanor
515 Clinton Street

# Make Your Own Happiness

In this life it is unhappiness that will find you.
It is happiness that has to be searched out
like a needle in a haystack.

Anthony, David, David
(grandsons and son)
122 Brunswick Blvd.

# Who is In Control?

Master yourself,
you are then
able
to master others.

Ryan, Briana, Tiara
(Tiara's friends)
Springville, New York

# Hart to Heart

Regardless of our significance
never make the assumption
we cannot be inconspicuous.

Tiara
122 Brunswick Blvd.

# Him Cool

But what good is it gon do?

Marc
122 Brunswick Blvd.

# Consumption

If you take time to care for immediate things,
    you can take care of them.
If you leave them alone,
    they will take care of you.

Lucritia Blount Herring (great grandmother)  Nathan (great grandchild)
122 Brunswick Blvd.

# Solidarity Confinement

A devastated life
is a life
without
love.

MaLulie, Tiara
Prince of Peace Church of God in Christ
669 Kensington

# Mother Nature

Life inevitably retrieves
everything
it gives.

Buddy, Junnie, Kenny, Ronnie
110 Timon Place

77

# How Do You Know?

GOD adds and multiplies
    and is the sum
    and the product of all things.
Satan divides and subtracts
    and is the quotient
    and difference of all things.

Paula, Angie, Joanna, Beedo, Bumbo, David, Munchie, Bryan, LaLa, GooGoo, MeMe,
Sonia, Candy, Marc, Barus, Rachel, NayNay, Poppy, Shelly, Ouchie, Buttons, George,
Audrey, Faith, Chuch-o, Clorisha, Carmen, Ruby, Floyd, Jennifer
Mamo and younger grandchildren, my nieces and nephews
First Shiloh Baptist Church

# Who's Doing the Thinking?

More important
than
what
you
think
of
me,
is
what
I think of myself.

Tiara Diamond Herring
122 Brunswick Blvd.

## Love Is the Seasons

Premeditated fall,
the perpetual shedding of the spirit.

Pretentious winter,
consumes and lays love to sleep.

Precipitant spring,

vehemently unearths a sexual upheaval.

Presumptuous summer,

apex of solitude of a sustained bliss.

University @ Buffalo

# Human Ecstasy

Mentally,
physically,
and
spiritually
fit.

Kenny, Lulie, Junnie, Rosie, Grandpa, Buddy, Fred, Edna, Eleanor
325 South Division Street

# When Looking, Back Don't Forget to Look Ahead

I saw her peek over her shoulder and give a little grin,
She looked at her with a beam of pride in her eyes.

How straight, erect she stood, stomach in, chest out, youth all aglow.

"Too bad old lady," and I saw her walk away.

I saw the old lady peek over her shoulder; head bent, eyes quite dim, hunchbacked and stooped over.

"Didn't think it could happen so fast," as the old lady walked away.

Julie Davis Eberhart, Eleanor C. Gayles Davis, Lula Lucritia Adams Gayles
Edna E. Weston Adams   Alice Miller Weston
Five Generations 1958
Front Room of 325 South Division Street

# Self

Don't say you love everybody
until you learn how to love somebody.

Junnie, Rosie, Uncle David, Buddy, Lulie, Uncle Peter, Edna, Eleanor
325 South Division Street

*Love*

Lula Lucritia Gayles Herring
The Hilton

When falling
    there is no balance.
Everything is off-kilter.
Therefore, there is no need
    to worry about stumbling
    because everything is unstable.

# Logic

When the lover with whom he has fallen in love with
changes in any shape, form, or fashion,
he begins looking for the effects
of what caused him to fall in love
with the one he just fell out of love with.

Lula and George Herring
122 Brunswick Blvd.

# The Hands That Rocked the Cradle

Inferior to men, only in physical strength
and that's debatable.
Superiority is in the sex
that can reproduce itself
an infinite number of times.

Steve, Stanley, Gree, Ronnie, Edward, Kenny, Mamo
Cape Cod

# How Can I Quit?

No power of my own is sufficient.
Outside sources only overwhelm me.

How can I quit?

Don't start.

Elder and Sister Herring

# ᴧⱱalk, Don't Run

Jennifer and Marc Herring
(daughter & son)
Salvatore's Italian Gardens

Love is delicate. If you fall into it
   you could fall completely
   out of it.
Love is mystifying. If you run through it
   you may miss it.
Love is precious. If you slip into it
   you might break it.
Love is sweet.
   If you overindulge you might get sick.
Love is designed
   to be enjoyed over a period of time.
Love has endurance.
   If you move too swift
   you may lose its longevity.
True love can last a lifetime.

# Man My Soul

Life given a thousand times
couldn't equip you
to take it again;
it's too heavy!

Brother George Herring, Sister Lula Herring
Salvatore's Italian Gardens

# Gentle Is the Moment

Jeannie, Anthony
(first and second cousins)
Salvatore's Italian Gardens

Soothing is the silence.
Pure are the thoughts
creatively reflecting
all the good you've wrought.
Set awhile.
Smile awhile.
Don't move.
You've had it rough, but you are tough.

# Give No Man Your Sanity, Soul, or Salvation

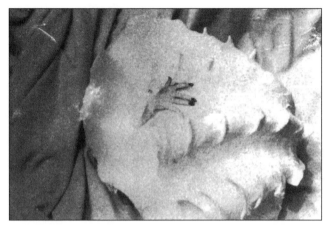

University @ Buffalo

You can't take it, I must give it.
There are some things I'm keeping for myself.
Give no man your sanity, soul, or salvation.
No one can implement them like I can.
Give no man your sanity, soul, or salvation.
I gave up mine, now I can't get it back.
Give no man your sanity, soul, or salvation.
I have lost something and now I feel cold.
Give no man your sanity, soul, or salvation.
No longer am I in control.
Give no man your sanity, soul, or salvation.
The master is now mastered because I gave
my sanity, soul, and salvation.

# Confusing

Who am I anyway?
Born in the world,
given a name,
taught to read and write.
Their being became my identification.
They found me or
I found them.
Each time I venture close
to discovering me,
I discover them.

Monique (niece)
122 Brunswick Blvd.

# He and I

He and I are like
two pieces of puzzles
that don't always fit,
yet are forced together
to fit smoothly.

Lula, George
Sho Gun Restaurant
Transit Road

For Good
or Evil

Kenny Hawkins, Steven Gayles

A successful person
dedicates their life
to one main purpose.

Kenneth Gayles, Jerry Livingston, David V. Herring, Bryan M. Herring
Lula L. Gayles Professional Center
480 Humboldt Pkwy.

94

# You Belong

Everybody is somebody's child.
Every man is not somebody's father.
Every woman is not somebody's mother.
Yet everybody is somebody's child.

Rocky
Kenneth Gayles II
Maple Road

Mama
Marian
325 South Division Street

# Waxed Cold

Love is a strange
and sometimes
a wonderful thing.
It has a life of its own
and feeds on substances
unknown to me.
Still, I would not trade it
for anything,
I know.

Clorisha, Faith (nieces)

# Confused

When I discover
who I am.
I may be able
to tell you
how I have gotten to be
the person I am.

Marc, Barus (nephew)
122 Brunswick Blvd.

# Holding Center

I have been told that I am free.
What does free mean '
when I am locked in a portable jail?
1975 I almost died physically.
1977 I died spiritually.

Lula

# 1+1-1-1=1

When I love me (1),
Then I can love you (+1).
When I love you alone (1),
I forget about me (1-1).
Therefore, the wise choice is. (1+1).

LaLa, GooGoo, Aunt Lulie, Oochie

# Looking for Love

When searching for love,
don't forget
to
look
inside
your own
heart.

Diane , La La, Alice
Channel 7, WKBW

# Too Selective

You get more mileage
out of love
when you
allow
yourself
the
opportunity
to
accept
love
the
way
it
is
offered.

Fred,  Stanley, Dr. Kenneth L. Gayles
Gayles Family Singers Anniversary
First Shiloh Baptist Church
15 Pine Street

# The Great Pretender

Skeletons in the closet
reflects a moment
of realism
then
we revert
to who people

think we are.

Bryan, Lula
First Shiloh Baptist Church
Pine Street

# Highs and Lows

Everyone looks for a high,
an escape from the mundane.
Religious people
find it in religion.
Chemically addicted people
find it in drugs.
The difference is
how each comes down after the high
and how frequently
each has to go
back up to the high.

Fred, Stephanie, Kenny
(niece)
110 Timon Street

# Together As One

All men try to prove their masculinity
during sexual intercourse.
The majority
fail to prove this.
Of those who fail,
they try other means.

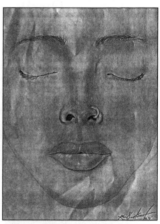

Artist  Marc Steven Herring

Some by condescending attitudes,
"Can't you do nothin' right?
The longer I stay wit you the dumber you git!"
Most by peer pressure,
"Man, you let yoe wife tell you
when you got to be home?"
All those forms prove
a void of intelligence in any man!
"I am me and she is she
and together as one,
is the way it should be."

Lulie, George,Bryan

# A Wealth of Loving Encroachment

A condescending wave of vigorous
    and lively abroached absolutism.
A debonair, intoxicating resource
    of overwhelming tenderness and sharing.
An enthrall of life's most
    reminiscent pleasures.
A desire of lust.
A secret, not secret anymore.
A cradle of caring.
An eloquent embrace.
An eruption of lusciousness.
A move of infinite exact fineness creating a
    homogeneous oneness.
Oneness that is indelible, impenetrable,
    and imponderable.

# Death Comes Creeping Like a Shadow

Totally unexpected
everyone else knew;
stood by and watched.
No one warned you it was coming.
However, you won't come back.
You are happy where you are
compared to where you've been.

Mamo
Buffalo General Hospital

# Can You See What I See?

Man often loves those
he should fight
and fights
those
he should love.

Maxi Gregg Adams  (Papa), Edna Weston Adams (Motha)(grandparents)
148 Adams Street

Be Yourself

Who and what
are the criteria
for the way we
act and react.
Actions determined
by others.
how we act
and how
others accept
our actions.
Actions determined
by one's self
without regards
of acceptance
or rejections.

Uncle Bennie, Cousin Wesley, Aunt Edna

**Forgive and Forget**

Life is too short
to remember slights or insults,
to cherish grudges
that rob us of happiness,
and miss making friends.
This place is too small
and we are too few,
there is something we all can do.
Let's bind together
the force of love
and put forth the effort
not to make living a drudge.
You are all appreciated
for the exceptional
work that you do.
Let's make life pleasant
for me,
you,
and you.

Nathan, Tiara
122 Brunswick Blvd.

# Exercise Thought

When I care what you think,
I do what you say.
When I think
not to care.
I do
what
I want.

Diyo, Naldo
325 South Division Street

# It Won't Last Forever

If machismo
is a man's
only expertise,
what will he do
when his
machismo
runs
out?

Uncle Bennie, Uncle John

# Leave the Door Open

Be careful whom you give your heart to.
They can adore, use, or abuse it.
They can value, cherish, or love it.
They can control your wants and wishes.
Those things that pleased or displeased
will become your thoughts and aims.

Maria Suarez, Dr. Kenneth Gayles
Lula Lucritia Gayles Center
480 Humboldt Pkwy.

Aunt Edna, Mama, Aunt Alice
122 Brunswick Blvd.

# Unforgiving

The first wound comes from the offender.
As a result:
I will tell everyone what happened.
I will never speak to her again.
I will never give her anything again.
I will never go to her house.
When I see her, I will walk the other way.
I will turn my back on her if I'm ever in her presence.
I get uptight when I see her or think of her.
When I get the chance, I will do the same thing to her
she did to me.
It's like a soldier who is wounded in battle who takes
his bayonet and began stabbing himself continually
wounding while the offender has gone and forgotten
the offense.
It's like being bound in a moment; the enemy has caused
life to stand still at an unusually painful point.
It's like heaping coals of fire on your own head.

# Unmotivated

If what is said is not controversial,
It is not worth saying.
There is no debate.
Everyone is in full agreement;
there is no room for change.

Marion, Edna, Diane
Buffalo General Hospital

# Sincerity

Pray without ceasing
asking of GOD only once.
We pray with our thoughts and
every action.

Professor Edna Earl Gayles Kee
Channel. 7 WKBW

# Actions Count

Lula Lucritia Adams Gayles (Mamo)
Alice Miller Weston (Maa)
Crystal Beach, Canada

Pay close attention
to every move you take in life.
Don't take any move for granted.
How you move today will affect
your tomorrow and your eternity.
Moreover, have an attitude of gratitude.

# Twenty Four Seven

Master yourself.
You are then
able
to
master others.

Kenny, Buddy
Reservoir State Part, Niagara Falls, N ew York

Faith

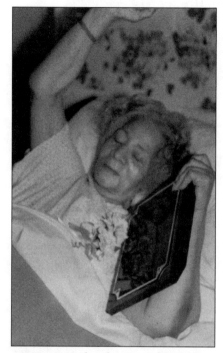

"Praise God in the name of Jesus!"
1984 Mamo @ Buffalo General Hospital
giving GOD the glory just before she died of cancer

It is
humanly
impossible to please
GOD.

# No Longer Twain

We pray as sweethearts that GOD would
direct our attention to do what he says.
Our mouth to speak what he says.
Our ear to hear what he says.
Our feet to go where he says,
and our heart to believe what he says.

Bryan, George, Lula

Roxie Lykes
great great aunt

Do That Again

History does not repeat itself,
we fail to learn from it,
history simply records our mistakes.

Thomas Miller
great great grandfather

Liza Miller
great great grandmother

1800's?   Charcoal drawings

# If You Slip, Don't Slide

It is no great sin to slip.
It is a sin if you go down and stay down.
Lust of the flesh, feels good!
Lust of the eye, looks good!
Lust of the pride of life, sounds good!

Be careful how you walk.

Lula
Forest Lawn Cemetery

# Don't Fool Yourself

Those who walk with their heads down
 are looking for something.
Those who walk with their heads up have found
it in Jesus Christ.

Steve, Gregg, Stanley, David, Beedo
Bennett High School, 2885 Main Street

*One GOD*

There are many religions.
Many denominations.
Many interpretations.
One form of worship,
those that worship HIM
must worship HIM
in spirit and in truth.

Marc, Bryan, David
"Now I lay me down to sleep. I pray the Lord my soul to keep."
122 Brunswick Blvd

Equality

Lula Lucritia Gayles Herring
122 Brunswick Blvd.

I am equal to everyone
And unequal to no one.

# Repeat or Defeat

Whatever the experience, learn from it.
Whether the experience is positive or negative,
learn from it.
Whether the experience is yours or someone else's,
learn from it.
If the experience is positive, learn how to repeat it.

OOH-B-Do, Nickie
Reservoir State Park,  Niagara Falls, New York

If the experience is negative, learn to defeat it by not
repeating it.

# It Looked Like the Snow Would Never Melt

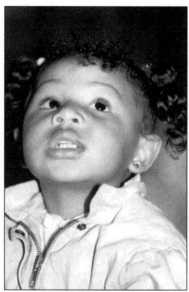

OOH-B-Do
122 Brunswick Blvd.

Looking from the backyard, it can't be done.
Take a look in the front yard and all possibilities
appear.
No one ever succeeded going forward looking back.

# Moving On

A total sense of uselessness
has overwhelmed me,
a temporal state at best.

Sonia (niece)
122 Brunswick

# First Things First

Love yourself,
put GOD first
then set out to conquer your world.

Marc Steven Herring
122 Brunswick

Not So Proud

There was some dark,
disgraceful, unpleasant days.
LORD, blot them
out of my memory.
More of THEE in "93".

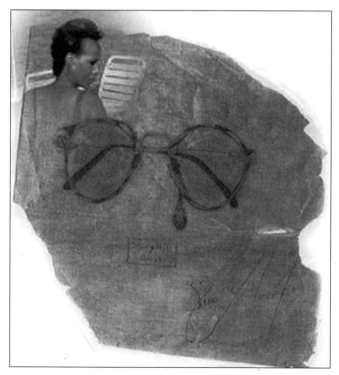

Cindy LuGal
Pocono's Cascade, New York

# Self Evaluation

To know yourself
is to look at yourself
in action with others.

Faith, Hanna, Clorisha (nieces)
Prince of Peace Church of God in Christ
669 Kensington Ave.

# Nonresident

Do not allow evil into your heart,
it will make a home there.

Edna Earl Weston Adams

# When You're Wrong

Don't waste time making
others agree with you
rather be more agreeable with others.

Iky, Bryan
(friend)
122 Brunswick Blvd.

# Nuts / Sharing

It's what's inside the shell
that can be eaten.

Mamo, Aunt Elizabeth, Uncle Joe
122 Brunswick Blvd.

Love isn't love until you give it away.

# He is GOD

Don't doubt GOD
because of man.

Lula Lucritia Adams Gayles (Mamo), Edna Earl Weston Adams (Motha)

## See

Good looks are good to have,

Bryan  Marc  Mama  David
Crystal Beach

but once you leave the mirror,
someone else is doing the looking.

George & Lula
122 Brunswick Blvd.

## Sweetheart

Sweet and sincere
wanting to please, tease, and not deceive.
Easy, because it comes naturally,
eternally, and without a doubt never ends.
I treasure sharing my life with you.
I give you heavy passionate
earnestly free and easy unadulterated love and care.
Rejecting and forsaking all others.
Trusting heart, mind, and soul to another.

Ronnie, Pam, Buddy, Collie
325 South Division

# Show the World You Can Hang

Show special pride and determination; you've shown success.

Keep pushing upward, with faith, trusting in GOD that you shall reap glory.

Yesterday a dream, tomorrow a vision of hope, believe in yourself, always remembering there's nothing you can't achieve.

No dream is too lofty, no goal is too high. The world's a brighter lovelier place because of your stride.

Hard work makes dreams come true. Let this moment be a hint of what's in store for you.

Success is what you make it and it's waiting for you.

# Truly Grateful

Enjoy life because the time may come:
When you have a car and can't drive it.
You may have a house and can't clean it.
You may have a phone and can't speak on it.
You may have a radio and can't hear it.
You may have a TV and can't see it.
You may have life and can't feel it.

Bryan, Marc, Chief (grandfather), David
110 Timon Street

# Going There, Can't Tell Been There, How to Get There

Candy, Aunt Lulie
122 Brunswick Blvd.

Children have manipulated us to the point that they are the parents and we are the children.
We say right, they say left.
We say no, they say yes.
We say go to school, they say go to hell.
Parents afraid of their own children.
Children go to school with dope in their veins and no hope in their brains.
Children used to hear Mama and Daddy praying. Now they hear them saying, "I hate you, I'll kill you."
Children may witness a slaying.
Parents need to take back the streets and take back the home.
Daddies need to go home and if given a choice mamas need to stay home.

# Sin

The soul of consciousness
has been removed
and the mind is anesthetized.

Lula
Montego Bay, Jamaica, West Indies

# Seeing Is Believing

Who and what are the criterias
for the way we act and react?
Actions and reactions determined by others
or actions and reactions determined
by one's self.

Star man, Ronnie, Kenny, Rocky, Beedo, Poppy
Ramsey, Maxy, Pharaoh, Contesa, Edna
Bumbo, Vivian
(sisters, brothers, nieces, nephews)

# The Search Is Over

Year after year
The reoccurring dream
Of fortune in the attic
Lingered in my sleep.
I searched the attic
High and low
From the ceiling
To the floor,
Found nothing but dust
And no fortune.
Once I unlocked the
Interpretation of the dream
I sat down and wrote a book,
There was a fortune,
It was found in my head.
You have a fortune in your head
It may not be a book,
But take the time

To look.

Jamaica, West Indies

# The Cost

Whether you truly don't know
or
intellectually select
not to know
ignorance has its price.

Lula, George

# No Bad News

If it's good news, I will rejoice.
If it's bad news, I will be sad.
If it's negative news, I have a choice.

Ronnie, Gregg, Steve, Stanley, Beedo
110 Timon Street

# The Bible

I hit the jackpot
It's JESUS, HOLY BOOK
My ship has arrived.
Jesus is my Savior,
I can ask what I want.
Not only do I gain heavenly eternal life
I also possess earthly treasures and wealth.

Daddy, Marc, Bryan
122 Brunswick Blvd.

# By Yourself

Vivian, Kenny, Edna, Diane, Marian,
Lulie, Alice, Pam, Gregg Ronnie,
Steve
110 Timon Place

Many women sing love songs that say, I don't have nothing if I don't have you.

Women, we have to stop singing these songs. Love is so strong that if you have love for yourself, you have confidence that if he walks away you do have something.

You were born in this world. With the exception of Mom's aid, you got here by yourself. When life ends, even though others may be dying, it ends with absolutely no one but you.

Thank GOD for family, friends, and acquaintances that come into our lives,

If you lose them all you can regroup and survive psychologically, physically, and spiritually because you possess the power to love yourself.

# Choose Ye This Day

If you will not
Have JESUS as your savior
You will have him as your judge

Uncle Bubba, Uncle John
Adams

# Incapable

When I am unable to decide for myself,
my brother is my keeper.

Aaron, Ronnie
(nephew)
Reservoir State Park, Niagara Falls, New York

# Giving Too Much

When another's happiness
decides my happiness
 I gave
 the power to do so.

Uncle  Marc, DaDa
122 Brunswick Blvd.

# Better With Age

What is it about the black woman?
Time makes her as fine as wine.
Time adds to her maturity,
honors her with beauty and grace
the young could not possess.
A stride with pride
that makes a man confess the black woman is the best.

Sister Livingston, Sister Suarez, Sister Gayles, Sister Johnson, Sister Herring
Prince of Peace Church of God in Christ

# Women Can't Preach

Do you believe Satan
can use a woman
to seduce
a man
into hell?
Then you must believe

Evangelist missionary Lula Lucritia Gayles Herring

GOD can
use a woman
to draw
a man
into heaven.

# Based on Knowledge

No matter who we are, we all act
and
react
according to
our acquired knowledge.

Gregg Joseph Gayles, Klunie
Prince of Peace Church of God in Christ

# Change

I can't change the world.
I can change my mind.

Tiara
122 Brunswick Blvd.

# Something to Think About

Have you ever stopped to think why Satan tempted Eve and not Adam?
Men think of the here and now.
Women think of the now and the future.

Man is satisfied with the here and now.
Women prepare for satisfaction now and in the future.
Man was satisfied with GOD, for it was GOD who saw him lonely and made him a helpmeet.
Women wanted wisdom, man, and GOD.

Evangelist missionary Lula Lucritia Gayles Herring
(Prince of Peace Church of God in Christ)

# Ten Steps to Connect with GOD

Pam, Alice, Buddy, Fred
Catholic Church
South Division and Cedar

1. Recognize I am disconnected with GOD (1 Peter 2:11).
2. Recognize the sin that disconnected me from GOD (2 Timothy 2:4,22).
3. Become godly sorrowful (John 8:32).
4. Repent and ask forgiveness from those I have sinned against (Romans 8:2).
5. Repent and ask forgiveness of GOD (Isaiah 51:11).
6. If the sin is a sin of torment, (a sin that the devil holds over me and won't allow me to forget), put the sin out of my memory until I can see my brother, sister or myself without shame or blame (James 4:7).
7. Get rid of anything physical or mental that would cause that sin to reoccur (Romans 8:6-8).
8. Pray to GOD for strength not to look, touch, or in dulge in anything that might cause the reoccurrence of that particular sin (Revelation 12:11).
9. Live a sainted life as though that sin had never occurred. Believe that sin is in the sea of forgetfulness and forget it! (Hebrews 2:9,14-15).

10. Ask GOD for forgiveness and thank GOD for forgiveness daily! Be careful for nothing! Read God's Word daily. Earnestly contend for the faith. Entreat my neighbor as myself. Know that I belong to GOD and not to myself. Realize that above all GOD loves me! (Ephesians 6:10-18 KJV).

# Forgive As We Forgive

My husband speaks

Dear GOD, in the name of Jesus,

I thank You for all the blessings, both spiritual and natural,

that You have bestowed upon my family and me.

The blessings of health, happiness, and most of all salvation.

However, I am lacking in many areas of my life.

In the name of Jesus, I ask for wisdom, knowledge, and understanding in all facets of life.

Help me to be more sensitive to the moving of Your spirit. Help me to make the necessary sacrifices in dedication, obedience, and in righteous living, whereby I might receive a mighty anointing and be able to demonstrate a great witness for the gospel's sake.

Teach me how to go in and out before You and people everywhere.

Teach me how to continually keep myself unspotted from the world.

Teach me how to overcome self in every aspect and give me the power through Christ to be an overcomer.

Most of all help me to be the man, the saint, the husband, the father, and the preacher that You would be most pleased with. Help me to recognize Your will and abide in it. Help me to let these words become more of a reality in the days to come than they are in the present. These petitions I make, in the name of Jesus.

Yours for a better son,

Elder George Diamond Herring Jr.

# Christmas Gifts

Poppy, Mamo
(nephew)

Gifts of gold, frankincense, and myrrh.
Day one
After praying, fasting, and resting, give someone
a gift to give to someone else.
GOD gave his only begotten Son.

Day two
Give someone you do not know a gift.
Tell them just as easy as it was to take the gift, it is as
easy to accept the gift of Jesus as their savior.

Day three
Do something for someone besides giving something
of monetary value. Owe no man anything but to love
him/her.

# Birthday Gifts

December 11, 2001,
I'm throwing myself a birthday party.
Everyone will receive his or her Christmas gift.
Everyone will bring a monetary gift for the poor people in foreign countries.
Everyone will bring seeds to be planted in a foreign country.
This is your gift to Lulie on her 60th birthday.
Happy birthday, every living soul.

# Cut Through the Chase

Direct,
lucid,
and

Buffalo, New York

simple
is my approach
to
communication.

# For the Moment

A sense of uselessness has overwhelmed me
a temporal state at best.

Buffalo, New York

Possibility?

If at first you don't succeed,
someone or something
may be standing in your way.

Artist, Marc Steven Herring

Infallible

Perfection
leaves no room
for human error.

Mamo, Sister Herring, Gayles Family Singers
122 Brunswick Blvd.

# Hidden Agenda

The more men oppress women,
the less visible men's limitation.

Buffalo, New York

# Chauvinistic

I have acquired a male ego.
It's not in the genes.
It's an attitude!

Lula Lucritia Gayles Herring
122 Brunswick Blvd.

# Undisturbed

The most important person to be at peace with is one's self.

Lula Lucritia Gayles Herring
Disney World, Orlando, Florida

# Selfish

If life was only what we thought
Life would not exist for anyone else.

Rochester, New York, I am in the hotel waiting to receive my Evangelist
Missionary license from the Church of God in Christ.
Notice the eye in the middle of the right side of the picture. Turn the picture
upside down and see all the people lined up for heaven.

168

# Comparison

In comparing there is always
a better or worse.
When analyzing for intrinsic value
the results stand alone.

122 Brunswick.

## Sounds Like Heaven to Me

Lula Lucritia Gayles Herring
Salvatore's Italian Gardens

If all the kings will become the subjects.
If all the accusers will become the accused.
If all the dictators will become the oppressed.
If all the politicians will become the public.
If all the rapists will become the raped.
If all the murderers will become the victims.
If all the K K K will become the Catholics, black men,
    homosexuals, and the Jews.
If all the child molesters will become the molested.
If all the cruel jailers will become the prisoners.
If all the false accusers will become the accused.
If all the rich will become the poor.
If all the jack-legged preachers will become the
    parishioners.
If all the johns will become the prostitutes.
If all the macho men will become the women.
Reincarnation? Sounds like heaven to me.

# My Brother's Keeper

With destruction all around
there is wisdom in the tornado.
After the storm, miraculously the storm has left
something totally intact.
Saved, knowing I survived the storm.
Saved, to assist the fate of others who were less
fortunate.
Think! In the midst of trouble
We must pray for ourselves
and more for others.

Sabana Grande LaBoya, Dominican Republic
At the left top of the picture, a face in the cloud.

# Rise Above It

Let every stumblingblock
be a stepping-stone.
let every knock be a boost.
Let every obstacle lead the way
to finish the course.

Humboldt Parkway

# Hold Your Peace

Do prepare for battle.
However,
victory is mine,
saith the LORD.

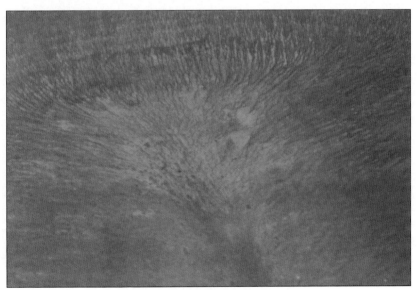

Bathtub picture: girl in the middle of the picture,
people lined up to go to heaven
122 Brunswick Blvd.

# Empathy

I cry when others cry.
Seldom do I cry for myself,
even then
the tears are for
someone else.

Lake Niagara

# All Things Work Together for the Good

Lady in the Bathtub
122 Brunswick Blvd.

Life is an orchestra
Playing every imaginable and unimaginable instrument,
but only GOD knows the score.

# It's About Time

1977 I started listening exclusively to heaven.
2000 into the Father, Son, and Holy Ghost!
2001 into the Father, Son, and Holy Ghost. Stand!
2002 LORD, I'm through. I've done what You told me
to do, Now I patiently wait for You to give me
something new to do!

Rochester, New York

# Which Way Do You Want to Go?

Bathtub image of doves,
cross, face, and people lined
up to go to heaven.

Like the salmon,
in order to bring forth new life,
you must go against the flow.
When you are in the mainstream
you get to see which way the river flows.
In order to save yourself and bring forth new life
you must go against the flow.

# Using the Appropriate Tool

It would take longer to cut down a tree
if the saw blade went in one direction only.

Foreign missionary Diane Livingston
Prince of Peace Church of God in Christ
669 Kensington Ave.

# Don't Lose the Opportunity

Be angry and sin not
for in not sinning
some soul you might
be winning.

Evangelist missionary Lula Lucritia Gayles Herring
Rochester, New York

# My Yoke Is Easy

Carry the cross,
not for the burden,
but
for the victory.

Missionary Diane Livingston
Evangelist missionary Lula Lucritia Gayles Herring
Presentation of the Sabana Grande LaBoya Mission
Prince of Peace Church of God in Christ

# Repeat or Not to Repeat

Learn two things from every person
moreover, every experience.
Learn what to do.
Learn what not to do.

Marc Steven Herring, George D. Herring

# Dedicated to God

Allen, Barus, Clorisha, Poppy, Faith,
Daniel, Mia, Hanna, Angelo
Ryan, Marion 166
(sister, nieces, nephews, great nephews)

I being a son of GOD
do dedicate my family
As children of GOD.
That their lives be dedicated to You.
Protected by your LOVE and guidance.
May life be GOOD to them.
May there always be someone there to love
respect and cherish them.
May an ANGEL of LOVE and GRACE forever shield
and protect them.
May their eyes see the GOOD.
Their minds strong enough to discern evil.
May they LOVE and hold themselves in HIGH ESTEEM.
May they forever seek WISDOM and KNOWLEDGE.
May their health and body
reflect GOD'S GRACE and GOODNESS.
May the love of GOD REST, RULE, and ABIDE in them
FOREVER.

Lula Lucritia Gayles Herring
It's Not About Me It's All About Thee

# About the Author

Lula Lucritia Gayles Herring, fourth oldest of seventeen sisters and brothers. As a young child, I lived in poverty. However, I never knew a day of hunger, neglect, rejection, gas or electric turned off, haunting bill collectors, shopping at the Good Will Industries, abandonment of a father or mother, lack of love, physical altercations with a brother or a sister, going without a roof over my head

I remember how Daddy worked at the Bethlehem Steel Plant in Lackawanna, New York for forty-five years, never missing a day of work, and bringing all but five dollars of his paycheck to Mama. I remember Mama not buying a dress for seven years so that the mortgage would be paid on 325 South Division and purchasing a home at 148 Adams Street for my grandparents and my great grandmother, Papa, Motha, and Maa.

Mama taught us three things I will never forget: put GOD first, education next, and be a good citizen. From this teaching all my brothers and sisters have a college education, are independent yet interdependent upon one another, and GOD is first and foremost in our lives.

At the age of seven I lost one of my favorite uncles. Each night I knelt to pray, I saw my Uncle David kneel and pray on the other side of the bed. Not once was I afraid of him. At the age of nine, I saw myself in a vision on the foreign field. At the age of twelve I saw my great grandfather who had passed walk into the living room and within minutes my great grandmother passed. At the age of fifteen my brother Edward and I were born again.

At the age of seventeen I had an experience of someone smothering me to death. The next day Mama and the police woke me and said a neighbor saw a man trying to break into my window. I have experienced the foreign fields, founder of a food bank at the Prince of Peace Church of God in Christ and taught Sunday school at the age of fifteen at the First Shiloh Baptist Church.

I have seen the skirts of heaven. God has revealed His will in me. I have seen Jesus offering me abundant life. I have seen angels. I have been told by GOD to tell a dead man to get up. I have been given the spirit of discernment. GOD said He gave me: power over the devil, power to pull down strongholds, and the utterance of the Holy Ghost. (see Ephesians 6:19 KJV)

I have had many experiences in my life, but the most rewarding is when I can give and show love. It is my philosophy that we are to achieve two things in this life and that is to love and be loved.

Evangelist, foreign missionary, actress, producer, director, recording artist, songwriter, composer, unpublished play—"The Preacher Wo/man", CD—"It's Not About Me, It's All About Thee"; "The Gayles Family Album"; "Stand America"; and many unpublished books and plays.

Wife of George Diamond Herring, mother of Bryan, David, and Marc Herring. Mother, by law, of Jennifer Shank Herring, Linda Melnick Herring, grandmother of Heather Melnick, Tiara Diamond Herring, David Vaughn Herring, and Nathan Cato Herring, fifty-six nieces and nephews and fifty-two great nieces and nephews.

# Picture Credits

Front cover: Lula Lucritia Gayles Herring
In Memory of: page III, Lula Lucritia Gayles Herring
Lady in the Bathtub: page XI, Lula Lucritia Gayles Herring
Introduction: page XIII, top- Lula Lucritia Adams Gayles
Introduction: page XXII, Lula Lucritia Adams Gayles
Introduction: page XVII, Diane Gloria Gayles Livingston
Introduction: page XXIII, David Richardson
Photographs by Lula Lucritia Gayles Herring: pages, 24, 25, 26, 27, 28, 29, 31, 34, 36, 38, 40, 41, 45, 46, 49, 50, 53, 54, 55, 56, 57, 59, 60, 61, 64, 67, 69, 71, 73, 74, 75, 77, 79, 80, 82, 88, 90, 91, 92, 94, 95,96, 97, 100, 101, 103, 104, 106, 108, 109, 112,113, 114,115, 117, 118, 122, 123, 125, 126, 127, 128, 130, 132, 133, 138, 141, 144, 145, 148, 149, 153, 157, 159, 161, 162, 165, 168, 169, 171, 172, 173, 174, 175, 176, 177, 178, 181, 182
Photographs by Lula Lucritia Adams Gayles: Pages, 30, 32, 33, (upper right and bottom left), 35, 47, 51, 66, 70, 81, 83, 107, 110, 111, 137, 146, 155
Photograph by Edna Weston Adams: page 116
Photographs by Ronald Leroy Gayles: pages, 37, 43, 86, 89, 99, 105, 119, 142, 150, 170
Photographs by Marc Steven Herring: pages, 52, 58, 63, 68, 76, 84, 85, 93, 102, 151, 164
Photographs by David Vaughn Herring Sr.: pages 42, 166
Photograph by Bryan Michael Herring: page 136

# Picture Credits

Photographs by George Diamond Herring Jr. pages 33, 48, 62, 124, 129, 139, 140, 160,

Photographs by Alice Velma Gayles Floyd: pages 152, 167

Photographs by Jennifer Schenk Herring: page 72

Photographs by Janet Muriel Herring Hamm: pages 87, 143

Photographer unknown: pages 31, 39, 65, 116, 131, 134, 147

Photograph by Denise Fanning, Rochester, New York: page 179

Sattler's at 998 Broadway: page 44

Photograph by David Richardson: page 78

Photograph by Coleen Dove: page 154, 180

Photo taken in a booth at Crystal Beach, Canada: page 135

Artist Marc Steven Herring: pages 104, 129, 163

Artist Marian Gayles Shaw: page 37

Charcoal drawing: early 1800's (?) page 120

About the Author: George Diamond Herring Jr.

All pictures taken in the city of Buffalo, New York, unless otherwise specified.

To order additional copies of

# These Women
# Better Get Smart

Please contact
## Selah Publishing Group
toll free in the U.S.
## 1-800-917-BOOK (2665)
or by e-mail at
## orders@selahbooks.com
or order online at
## www.selahbooks.com
or
## Lula L. Herring
## PO Box 776
## Buffalo, NY 14209
or
## e-mail malulie@msn.com